Wren Cantata

Annie Deppe

SUMMER PALACE PRESS

First published in 2009 by

Summer Palace Press

Cladnageeragh, Kilbeg, Kilcar, County Donegal, Ireland

and

31 Stranmillis Park, Belfast BT9 5AU

© Annie Deppe, 2009

Printed by Nicholson & Bass Ltd.

A catalogue record for this book is available
from the British Library

ISBN 978-0-9560995-5-6

This book is printed on elemental chlorine-free paper

for Ted
and for Michael, Peter, Caitlin and Ben

Acknowledgments

Some of the poems in this book have appeared in: *Poetry Ireland Review*; *The Stinging Fly*; *The SHOp*; *Sou'wester*; *Babel Fruit*; *Sojourners Magazine* and *Landing Places: Immigrant Poets in Ireland* (an anthology edited by Eva Bourke and Dr Borbála Faragó, 2010).

Biographical Note

Annie Deppe was born in Hartford, Connecticut, and is a dual citizen of Ireland and the United States. She is the author of *Sitting in the Sky* (Summer Palace Press, 2003). Her work has been anthologized in the *Forward Book of Poetry 2004* (England). She has received a title-by-title individual grant from the Irish Arts Council and was selected by Poetry Ireland for their Introductions reading series. She works for Stonecoast in Ireland (part of the University of Southern Maine's Stonecoast MFA programme), as well as creating and running independent writing conferences, facilitating workshops, and as a freelance copy editor and writing mentor. She lives on the west coast of Ireland.

CONTENTS

The Sacrament of the Bees	11
The Good Daughter	13
A New England Childhood	14
Silver Belle	16
The Orchard	18
Brown Paper Packet	19
Joshua at Six	21
Shelter	23
Midsummer	27
Cheek to Cheek	28
After Emergency Surgery	30
Benign	33
Losing a Year to Illness	34
Mardi Gras Letter from Falmore	35
Not Sure How, So Singing It Both Ways	36
Hairpins	38
The Glass Bell	39
Stirring the Pot	41
Cait	42
Lucca	43
Amsterdam, Two Visits	44

The End of May	45
Erato	48
The Tempest	50
Snapshot, Collioure	52
Wandering, Crete	53
All Saints' Night, Krákow	55
Salt	56
Buying the House	57
On the Lake Road Out of Maghery	58
Lucky Child	59
Family Portrait	60
Tonight We Make the Paper House	61
Irises	63

The Sacrament of the Bees

After my father died, no, I mean *later*,
after my mother died, there was the problem
of family treasure no one wanted.

What does it mean that we tossed out
a whole wall of boxes – a lifetime's work –
of his eloquent handwritten sermons?

Brothers, sister, we all divided things up,
chose which inheritances
we would carry forth. The thing is

somewhere in the midst of all that judgment
those penned words
may have held the sweetest and best

of that complex man. Still, it seems
none of us wanted to shoulder
the weight of all those lessons.

One morning in August I watched
from the chicken coop roof, tar
softening beneath my knees,

as my father opened the battered beehive
behind the apple tree in the garden:
an act I only got to witness once.

My brother was with his chickens
while my mother moved slowly
through morning chores, so only

an idle six-year-old was there to watch
as Father emerged from the barn,
white sleeves rolled down, bleached

trousers tucked, and his veiled helmet
like something my mother
would wear to church. August,

and even so early in the morning
the heat made my father appear
to shimmer in shades of white

against the corn as he squeezed a cloud
from the tip of the tin bee-smoker
then pried loose the hive's great lid.

Did amber flow that day
or was the colony already lost?
Whether he spoke then to the living

or the dead, he was murmuring something
to that hive, something that is lost now,
something we are poorer without, and freer.

The Good Daughter

I lied to my father and the lie
was like a bus pulling away
from the station, and when
the headlights led us into night
the darkness was like sharing
first coffee, and when the cup
was empty we'd fill it again
and it was white like a coverlet
lifting over shy limbs,
and when those arms and legs
began to fly it was like
the dreaming heart of a circus,
like the taste of pomegranates
broken open,
like the imaginary chest of drawers
where everything finally fits.

A New England Childhood

Because her father is the minister
she has the old graveyard to play in.
She learns to count to one hundred
patting stone slabs the way her teacher
taps each child's head.

Among the stone angels
there's a song she is singing
about her birthday. She knows
March 18th is special,
part of what makes her *her*.

There's a door in the hillside
which opens
to empty shelves and a smell
like snow. There is nothing
in there. Odd to be scared of nothing.

But, in the cemetery's centre,
there's a long, raised grave that's safe
to lie on. Old stone raised like a table.
She likes to push bread crusts
into the dark between the cracks.

Willow is the name of the woman
down the hill. *The yellow
of the weeping* and *the yellow
of her hair* weave a sad
but strangely pleasing song.

There's a song she rises on
the way she does at night
when she floats higher
than Woodstock Hill
with its steeple and Pink House,

the town growing smaller,
it's a song
that frightens her
but she keeps on singing,
liking the lift of it.

She is five. She is singing.
Tomorrow she turns six.
She sings a little louder, hoping
her parents will hear her,
hoping they will know where she is.

Silver Belle

The summer I was six, my father rented Silver Belle –
a round, ill-tempered pony who liked to bite. Despite
being the youngest, I was the only one who could ride her.

She used to buck and send my brothers flying.
I liked the view from Silver Belle's broad back; it was as though
I'd come into my true height five feet off the ground.

Who was watching out for me the day of the summer haying? –
my tall hay playhouses cut and fallen,
the tractor and baler travelling in ever smaller circles,

Silver Belle beneath me stubbornly cropping
when the machinery's racket abruptly stopped
and from the far field where the foxes sometimes played

came a shout: my brothers needed a crowbar
to fix the baler. And then we were trotting over golden cuts,
Silver Belle and me riding out over remnants of grass houses,

trying to deliver the iron bar when it slapped
by accident against Silver Belle's neck
and who would have believed that fat pony could bolt so fast,

take off over fields and up the road
past the convent of the Sisters of the Holy Ghost,
hoofs clattering on the black tarmac, my brothers

running now too, though I couldn't see them,
only the saddle horn, don't let go of the saddle horn,
until the pony, winded, finally slowed.

My brothers arrived first and then my sister
driving the green station wagon
to bring your body home she told me later.

And where were our parents?
It's taken years for me to place that afternoon
into the August of my father's heart attack.

When the pony ran, it was hospital
visiting hours, and we four were left on our own.
Turning for home down Route 169,

maple leaves over our heads like a celebration of flags
and the unruly pony now docile,
we must have made a rag-tag parade

as we passed the gathered black-habited nuns,
my sister driving slowly
while one brother followed with Silver Belle,

leading her back to a rented pony's destiny
of always being returned, and bringing up the rear
my other brother with me perched high on his back,

his sweaty white tee-shirt prickly with hayseeds,
one of my arms wrapped around his sunburned neck,
and everyone waving, everyone waving.

The Orchard

No one told her of the baby they named Anne
so *Grandmother* became a lullaby

left outside at night. After she became the day
when the teacups dropped, no one spoke of her.

She was a room down a corridor I could not find
so why wouldn't I think she ran a brothel?

If *Grandmother* is the thief who travels in the night,
perhaps she is also the silver beneath the olive leaves.

Picture her as candlelight reflected in glass
or the charred letter lifted from a fire –

how did my handwriting come to resemble hers?
She is the apples never gathered.

Missed phone calls and a calendar of marked-off days.
Just a few windfalls scattered beneath the tree.

Brown Paper Packet

It was like a brown paper packet
handed down one generation to the next.

If only it had been something as easy as
a father who liked to dress as a woman. Instead
it was like something large
running in the walls at night,
like lightning trapped within the house.

My mother used to say
Just don't lose one another.
From my father's side and from my mother's,
loss handed down as though
wrapped in brown paper.

*Don't lose one another. It's too easy
to lose the people you love.*
This, a legacy from both sides of the family.

Always, it seemed, each generation,
one who disappeared.

From both sides.

I tried to change that, tried out words
that encouraged,
emboldened. Instead,

this flood of loss, this flood.

There were only two ways
to fit my bed into the room.

I tried them both, but either way
something scratched above me in the walls.

My mother passed down brown paper words
to the girl who was me
It's too easy, be careful, don't lose one another ...

I had to keep my feet from dangling
over the edge. I had to lie
so flat that when the murderer
came, I'd be invisible.

Joshua at Six

You were too distracted to sit still
and no one knew what to do with you,
so we were sent to work together
in the school's storage closet.

That first morning we carved out a space
between stacks of steel chairs,
mismatched desks and the new floor-waxer.
Then for weeks, we tried to find our way

through a wilderness of letters. Sometimes
you wept with frustration, so once
we let the papers slide to the floor
and played our own game tracing shapes of letters

on each other's back.
It must have taken everything you had
to calm yourself
and draw those constellations.

I wish now I'd filled that wasteland
with posters: Brueghel, maybe, with hunters
returning through a wintry world
like the hills of Western Massachusetts.

Or one from my study of
Winslow Homer's *Blue Boat* with its
two guides gliding through the backcountry.
Hunting and boats. Those you already understood.

But you'd also need
letters and words in the larger world.
Joshua, you must be nearly grown now,
and probably you've forgotten me,

but perhaps there still remains
a trace of the morning
when a listing ship of a bull moose
navigated the playground on awkward legs,

that giant, with its too-small head,
drifting sideways just beyond the slide,
and how you were the bravest boy
in school that day, drawn as you were

towards that shaggy beast.
How I had to wrap your shirt tails
around my fists to hold you fast. How you
were the boy humming the letter *m*.

Shelter

1.

In the harbour's new shop,
      a place geared
towards tourists, I find
      a crate of etchings

made by a woman
      from the next island.
In one, a small stone house
      hunkers

under a black onslaught
      of diagonal cuts.
This one interests me,
      I tell the girl

who minds shop. *The one*
      with the night? she asks.
But what I see is lashing rain.
      Is March storm. Is

shelter in a howler
      of a gale. I want
to show you
      but you are up the hill

trying to finish a poem
      of how we almost
lost each other
      in our own black spring.

2.

When we were twenty,
    to escape
our landlady's eyes
    we bicycled

out of Sligo and camped
    above Lough Gill.
We rigged a plastic sheet
    for shelter.

Two things I remember
    from that night:
the way we woke to find
    the full moon

beneath which we'd earlier
    made love,
eclipsed
    to a rust red ring,

and how by morning
    our sleeping bags
were drenched
    despite the plastic sky.

3.

Something in me
        doesn't understand
why, instead of my friend, I'm here
        walking past his home.

The same March day I drifted
        on the operating table in Boston,
this island friend died.
        I'd been back on Cape Clear

almost a week
        before I felt ready to wander
through knee-high grass
        looking for his grave.

4.

Last year
    I couldn't comprehend
why every poem I wrote
    seemed ringed by death.

After our old dog Seamus
    died, I hoped
those poems would stop.
    Summer evenings

when our children were young
    we'd set up elaborate games
of croquet. Seamus
    would crouch on the sidelines

trembling with excitement
    until, no longer able to stand it,
he'd swoop through
    and make off

with someone's wooden ball.
    For the length of the game
we renamed Seamus *Fate*,
    and if he took a ball

and ran with it
    we had to play it where it lay.

Midsummer

Her first day visiting the island,
my husband's mother tells me
the body remembers everything.
If this is true, what

was delivered from me
this spring, wrapped in that cyst,
the size of a newborn?

For weeks now, clumps of hair
pulling loose each shower.
Anaesthesia's toll. The dread
of brushing.

After a late supper,
my mother-in-law gazes
at the cows from our kitchen window.

Her chemo done. No wig. Elegant,
as though pared down to bedrock.
The cows as curious of us
as we are of them. New growth,

new growth. And the terrible play
of light and dark. The island
at dusk. Her face

mirrored in the window. The cows
leaning closer, pressing broad, black noses
against the glass, before wandering
away into gorse-lit fields.

Cheek to Cheek

Almost sundown, late September,
and though the moon's not yet full
a flood tide extends far into the reeds.
It's been half a year
since I floated on the operating table.

All my life I've feared surgery –
strange then to find those hours
the easiest part of the illness.
Such a sense of divine nothing.
If death comes like that,

it might not be so bad.
For days after the operation,
I'd close my eyes and feel the bed
vibrate and begin to rise.
At first I thought it was the morphine,

but even weaned I felt
that vibration turning into humming
then the humming into tune,
and I'd wake up singing
dancing cheek to cheek.

This evening, while taking
the last swim of the year,
I float in salt water, the sounds
of the world muffled
and the borders blurring,

enjoying the feel of body turned into
its own small boat, feet into the wind
and face to the sun. Above the cove,
an osprey, its underbelly
glowing in late light, hovers silently

and the song
floods back and once again
we are dancing, the words
falling into place, *I'm in heaven,
I'm in heaven.*

Good, now, to be surrounded by water
and the nourishment of light. Still,
there is something I miss
about that time when I was lifted,
almost literally, by a song.

After Emergency Surgery

Cradled in rare blue light
        the island spreads out

below. I didn't think I'd be able
        to return this year,

but here is the house
        with its stone table

and the sudden pheasant
        with its surprising red crown

and the cows' black flanks
        shimmering

in early Irish summer.
        Sounds of children

swimming in South Harbour,
        and all the while

a smell of scythed hay
        mixing somehow with lavender.

Sometimes
        I think of the soul

as a winged visitor,
        wandering here, then out of view.

Who made the painting
> that hangs in the Louvre

just to the right of Giotto's
> *St. Francis Preaching to the Birds*?

In it an angel kneels,
> offers Mary a lily

as he rends
> her life.

Each word a miracle,
> but it's the riffs of plumage,

the rainbowed wings,
> that steal the show,

as if the painter
> could not restrain himself,

as if paradise
> were a tropical island

which he'd once
> caught sight of.

A farmer burns gorse
> at the end of the Bill,

black-backed gulls glide
> through the plumes

but just beyond
> against the background

of blue, a single sail
> fills with light.

I travelled that way myself
> this spring,

lay rocking in bed
> as my boat rose,

the vibrations of something
> I could not see

keeping me company
> throughout the night

though I remember
> no birds, or angels.

But there was something
> like a sail –

no paradise,
> not even a lily –

something, like
> the trembling of a sail.

Benign

Just one of the little rehearsals we get
that makes me grateful
to be here this afternoon

walking through unbroken snow
past red haw berries and birches
with their soft blazes of lichen.

Last night I dreamed my dead father
came to me, sat on the edge
of my bed but I said *No,*

I want you to leave. He nodded –
Ach, Anne, you are alive again –
and retreated up the stairs.

Almost home, a sudden release
of heavy silver from the copper beech
as somewhere a cardinal calls.

I had forgotten the amaryllis bulb
dreaming the colour red
beneath the kitchen sink.

Losing a Year to Illness

Around the bend, I come on a story
spelled out in hoof prints
of how a doe must have leapt the snow bank,
only to have legs sprawl beneath her
when she landed on the storm-slicked road.

The good news of the year is this:
she scrambled to her feet and continued,
maybe even bounded a little, sharp tracks
clear beneath the weeping cherry,
its branches blooming with fresh March snow.

Mardi Gras Letter from Falmore

With these lines, I send you today's good light
glistening off the headland's quartz
and the slow white rise of herring gulls spiralling up

like drifts of ash from my neighbour's chimney.
It's been three years now since death
whispered my name, my body's pale fields

poisoned from within. As I write these words
I worry that nothing in my soul has changed
after escaping that slow descent into a place like ruin,

yet somehow yesterday's storm and
today's sun seem bound together. My neighbour
on his tractor passes through the steel gate,

spikes a massive bale wrapped in black plastic,
trundles it along the narrow lane to his waiting cows:
muddy-hocked but filled with expectation,

they parade through stony fields that glint
above the sea, while beyond them
red calves race along the sunlit cliffs.

Not Sure How, So Singing It Both Ways

Last night the *sean-nós* singer,
hands before her, sang
a slow Donegal air,
eyes closed, fingers
rising and falling
like the notes of her song
or the way thrush feathers
flutter when lifted
by wind off the Atlantic
until, towards song's end,
her hands hovered a moment
then rested against her breast.

I can't get that gesture
out of my mind as I walk
the cliff road around Crohy Head.
It's warm for November
and the sea is shifting below
like silver releasing light.
I find I'm remembering
how years ago a choir director
instructed us to not
close our eyes while we sang
but instead to meet the gaze
of each person before us
and minister to them.
There were times
when the gospel songs
appeared to shimmer
and expand until they
transfigured everything.

So now I pause along the road
and for a short time sing
with my eyes closed –
just long enough for the music
to expand unexpectedly within.
Next I try walking and singing
with my eyes wide open
and find everything
pressing outwards, blessing
anyone who can hear
in this world or the next,
even the choughs
sweeping past the place
where firm ground ends,
tumbling in the updraughts
for the joy of it.

Hairpins

Last week my sister said she threw out
the last of our dead mother's nightgowns.
For a decade, she'd slept wrapped in grief.

In our house, Mother's hairpins regularly appeared
on pantry shelves or under the oriental rug.
When we moved to Ireland I'd thought they'd stop,

but this morning I found another,
a stowaway, which crossed the ocean
in a journal, posing as a bookmark.

It holds the place where I wrote
about my neighbour's pet, blind Beatrice,
a sealed-eyed old cat

still the size of the kitten abandoned by its mother,
and how my friend emptied her drawers
to blanket three flights of stairs with clothes

and made a kind of ramp for Beatrice.
I almost take the hairpin out
to place upon my bureau like a little shrine.

The Glass Bell

Winter arrives early to this house above the sea.
November gales filled with sleet
blast the western windows, so as darkness falls

mid-afternoon I wonder how the new red calf
will survive the night. Ten years ago
we sold the family home

and since I'm the only one who's never gone back
to see what the new owner's changed,
for me the door latch still rattles

at the bottom of the stairs and the soft tick
of the mantel clock goes on as though I am tucked in
sick on the daybed in my father's study

with a glass bell left at my side.
In the field the calf romps by its mother,
staying close. Strange how the books I loved best

were all about children surviving alone:
in boxcars, in barns, in a burnt-out tree,
in the ruined rubble of war-torn Warsaw.

Now across Gweebarra Bay, last light
falls on the deserted village from whose strand
I once carried a rock across the Atlantic

to use as a door stop.
But that was yet another house.
The question of seas, of how that inner place

of feeling completely at home can be cleaved
clear through. When we sold our parents' house
we took turns choosing furniture and keepsakes

then let the rest of it go.
Betrayals like this can be explained,
but not to the girl who often refused

to clean her closet for fear of hurting the feelings
of what she'd throw out.
I miss the lilacs and white clapboards now,

my mother's maple desk,
even the sound of the bell
which once could call my mother to my side.

Stirring the Pot

After a night of broken sleep –
our teenage daughter disappearing
into the night with a boy we've never met,
someone we only know as Rufus – *Rufus?* –

my friend tells me, *Whatever
you do, don't isolate yourselves.
We promised our daughters
we'd be discreet. It almost killed us.*

So I try speaking out. I talk to the soup pot:
I'm feeling helpless. And the soup says,
*We're all in it together, dear. It's only
going to get hotter, lots hotter, before it's done.*

As I wash the dishes, I ask the mallows,
What should I do? They answer, *Dress yourself
in pink, darling, then sway, sway,
you're dancing the great fandango.*

And when the door opens and shuts
and I hear her steps
disappearing up the stairs,
I ask the door for its advice.

It thinks for a moment and says,
*Just don't lock me,
don't lock me, leave her a way back in,
babycakes, leave her a way back home.*

Cait

The universe is made of stories, not of atoms
         Muriel Rukeyser

The smell of oils. She must be
up on the sleeping porch, a tin lamp pinned
to a rafter for light, painting again.

One night when she was six,
she took from our living room
the Käthe Kollwitz etching
of an old woman clutching a basket

and hung it – as if by birthright – beside her bed:
*She's there to catch my nightmares
and put them in her basket.*

A grown woman now, Cait
wears her hair like Kollwitz
in long, thick braids coiled
upon her head – safe from wind
and the tyranny of the palette.

If you come to the foot of the stairs
you can hear her murmuring to the canvas.
She's asking her people their stories
as she brings them into life.

Lucca

A grace of green, the underleaf
of olive, the birdsong's
cradling. It's as though

something in us already knows
these blossomed streets,
her plane trees dappling,

the unfolding light
as children play hide-and-seek
outside the church.

We've found a place with
lanes that curve, with circling walls,
and a hidden piazza at the heart.

O mio babbino caro.
Ours is the window
of music that comes despite

death's green cave.
In this fleeting paradise,
a shop door opens

and Puccini soars
above baskets of artichokes
and blood oranges.

Amsterdam, Two Visits

Canals with their houseboats. The way chocolate
is served with breakfast. All this as I recall it,
but why can't I remember her hiding place?

My mother swears we went there. It almost comes back –
were the narrow stairs steep and blond, twisting to the left?
No, nothing is like it was then. Now I ascend

as if for the first time to rooms breathless with grief.
A film clip catches a dark-haired girl
leaning from the window, calling

to her parents to come and see, or perhaps
it is Margot she wants: a wedding party is leaving
as bicycles glide past the apartment house

and three sedans topped with luggage turn the corner.
The curled leaves fallen from the chestnut.
The leaves of her papers, rescued from the floor.

Everything falling: a mountain of shoes, stacks
upon stacks of luggage, this emptiness that every frame
seems to deny. I'm Anne and I'm eleven

and my mother is handing me a book. The girl on the cover
looks a bit like me with eyes that may be nearsighted too.
Perhaps she'll soon need glasses. And along with that girl

I fall for her Peter, so her first love
becomes my first dream of love.
A second visit and I'm standing with the two of them

at the attic window. I'm Annie now, and Anne still –
watching seagulls slide like the leaves of the chestnut.
How could I not choose Peter as my first son's name?

The End of May

After a month of dreadful
Irish weather – sleet, wind,
and cataracts of rain –
sleep eludes me tonight:

the duvet's too heavy
for the warmth
which has come at last.
I read for hours,

only half-aware
of the blackbird's song
beyond the window,
and find it strange –

having moved worlds
to come and live
on this island – to take
such comfort

in Richard Ford's
descriptions of
everyday life
in Haddam, New Jersey.

Morning now
and when I walk out
in my nightgown
to see if the neighbour's cow

calved last night, I find
the air swirling with thousands
of black bugs
motoring along like

miniature humming birds
out for a Sunday drive.
Who are they? Shinier
than the mud daubers

of my childhood
and smaller, their bodies
are like double beads
of antique jet

fitted out with full-length
wings: elegant
see-through affairs,
fine as organza.

I'm drinking coffee
with my husband
when I feel something
many-legged

crawl along my thigh,
so I shake my nightgown
and one, no, two
stowaways, still coupling,

fall end-to-end.
The larger pulls the other
backwards
onto the oil landscape

left by our daughter
to dry on the floor.
There they wander
over the red-blossomed

hedge at the end of the garden
and into the field
where Polo and her colt
sprint half-ghosted in mist.

Wanting to spare
these awkward
insect lovers, I carry them
outside on the painting

and deposit them
under that same
escallonia hedge.
Still they don't separate

but cling together
as they amble into the bower,
these diaphanous
yet stalwart travellers.

Erato

Like an osprey wheeling
over the silvering cove,

its cries piercing
the evening's heat.

Like bright summer blades,
white breast sliding sideways

above the meadow's
thistledown and flashing finches.

Like an invitation to come and float
above the shifting.

Then the sudden fold
and plunge, its talons spread

to part the cove's silk skin,
and like revelation, it lifts

its prize like light from water.
Almost perfect

the way desire approaches
with a swirl and flourish,

the hovering of wings
around the waking edge,

and in the sudden arch and lift
something within me rising

in carelessness
and golden disarray

to a place of flight
and sun-struck thistle seed,

and though longing
is never finally satisfied

and we'll have to create again
this dazzling palace

of levitation and light,
for now it's all

circling feathers
and tug and pull

and salty flanks
and sweet release.

The Tempest

When it storms on Crohy Head
and spray howls like torn smoke
through the sea-arches below the cliffs,

I sometimes think it's the dragon
stirring beneath us again. A few times
we've had to link arms to keep our footing.

I always believed our dragon
was good fortune, refusing to acknowledge
its twin of destruction.

Not so long ago, on a November night
filled with blowing snow, we stepped into
a café in Kraków, drawn

by candles and the way everyone
seemed to be leaning towards one another
deep in talk, music and smoke.

Leaving that city (named
for a dragon slayer) we returned
to learn of autumn storms which blew in

our neighbours' window. *When wind comes in,
it must go somewhere*, and if they hadn't been home
to board it up, the roof might have sailed away.

We once owned a house like that –
a former parsonage in Abington
where, decades before us,

a storm broke in and the roof rose
and spun across town to the cemetery.
Maybe the parson's wife took her eye

off her marriage. In that house, I could still hear
the inner weather fly down stairs and curve
through the hall, into the room of the living.

Snapshot, Collioure

Late afternoon and the dirty
white walls of Collioure's back streets
are warmed to the same pink
as the flowers we've stolen
for Antonio Machado's grave.
An Andalusian in France, his boat
forever *tied to another shore.*

The elderly couple from Barcelona
we met earlier in the market
have brought their dog to Machado's grave.
They're taking turns
pushing a baby buggy
with the raggedy spaniel stretched out within.
He's on ice, they explain, as they flip back
the blanket. *His hips are shot,
but he does so love to see the world.*

Wandering, Crete

The day is generous, and beneath dusty olive trees
we watch sheep wandering like Jacob's flocks

washed in gold. And when we come upon
a small stone church we find an icon of the two

saints Theodore. In gilded robes
they ride their horses side-by-side.

One Theodore smiles slightly,
the other wears a faint hint of a frown, perhaps

unable to find peace in this world.
On the slopes above: snow-pink cherry trees

and banks of beehives painted blue.
My father once kept bees. Bearded iris

edged his hives like dreams.
Now, on the slow journey back to the coast,

up and over the evening hues of mountains,
somewhere on the high lonely road

between Gerakari and Spili,
beyond white horses and tolling bells,

we enter a village and stop to stretch
beneath a dangling, misspelled sign:

Rooms for Rent
Food-Drings
Café-Sweetly
Cherrys

And though we'd only meant to stay
the length of a coffee

taken on a terrace with its valley view,
we linger at the wobbly table

as children play in the road
and beyond the blue shuttered door

garlic sautés and a woman laughs and
a family's enviably ordinary life goes on.

Sky blossoms and *Sweetly Cherrys*.
It's been a long time since I've felt

this much at home. It's good
to dwell here again, however brief the stay.

All Saints' Night, Kraków

A blind man and his three tall daughters pass us,
their gold lanterns falling and rising in thin snow,

gold lanterns like small boats, or like the notes of a song,
gold lanterns carried on wind, an elusive

music we follow down cobbled streets to a churchyard
where the daughters are adding their lights

to a winter sea of coloured lamps, glassy and jewel-toned.
Little candles. Little hymns. Little boats

arranged on low walls, going nowhere,
and at the same time setting off towards the dead.

Salt

What comes back now are fast walks on Falcarragh's back strand,
the sand no longer firm beneath our feet, and plovers
chasing each other in and out of the rolling edge.
Long talks of how we must one day leave everything.

Evenings, that winter, we read Akhmatova's poems aloud
and the city of Saint Petersburg filled our sitting room.
And once, when we stepped outside, the stars were the stars of Russia
and we remembered a friend who somehow resembled her:

that proud head, at times wrapped in a turban
to show off her long, Modigliani neck. Two lives
lived with the same passion, but one with reckless speed.
Paper. Salt. Stars. When are the sands ever firm?

Buying the House

Once I leaned against the newel post
at the bottom of the stairs and thought

This house will help protect me from life's pain.
I was very young and it would be years more

before I read how Bishop's moose
was *safe as a house.*

When the ER doctor told me, *Without a doubt
you have cancer ... and it has spread,*

he delivered his news so bravely.
The doctor, too, was young:

there was no cancer. And though I loved
the sense of safety those walls once lent,

the space they gave to start to dream,
in the end there was no house.

On the Lake Road Out of Maghery

After a phone call with our youngest son
in which he described his home above Willow Creek
as *an orchard by the sky,*

I walk the lake road out of Maghery,
watch cygnets try their wings,
long feet skimming then lifting

from that radiance.
If I had to say where my heart dwells now,
one answer would be *in pieces*

with my far-flung family,
but another might be, *along this marshy stretch*
of restless reeds and swans.

Neither firm land, nor water.

Lucky Child

My mother's giving birth
in a Chinese restaurant with people laughing
and blue platters scattering rice and noodles
and the hiss of steam boilers
mixing with tinny wind-up birdsong,

while out on the streets of Hartford
insurance forms blizzard down
and snowploughs roll. O wonderful city
of welcomes, where four wooden cherubs
guard the corners of Mark Twain's bed

and thirteen blackbirds sing in the cedar-limbs!
O pulse of red, I'm busy being born
as neon light falls in on me
and flashes the tiger: *good food, eat, eat* –
flashes the dragon: *good food, eat.*

Family Portrait

Out on the broad stone porch, Great Aunt Susie
eats her Sunday lunch without a sound, until, mid-meal,
she stands, looks around, and demands, *Where
is my hat? It's almost time to catch the tram!*
This, surrounded by Minnesota horse fields, twelve hundred miles
from Newark's inner city, several decades from Aunt Susie's
darkened, upstairs flat. The uncle who scares me
orders her, *Sit down and be quiet.*

After Susie dies, Grandma lives alone with only a donkey
to keep her company. Sometimes my father goes to visit.
He schedules it like business. One time he tells of
having to rescue Grandma from the bath.
Another time, how he heard from his bed a bell,
like a tram's, clanging in the cold Minnesota wind.

Tonight We Make the Paper House

Tonight, surrounded by a chorus
of Japanese maples and their bat-winged leaves,

my sister and I make the paper house, construct
room after room beneath the stars

until a kind of playhouse dangles
from a fallen branch. I say we make the house

but other hands also fashion these tiers of rooms
mixing brilliant paper with the bronzy calls

of peepers rising from the swamp.
After you died, Mother, we had to break

apart your home. So tonight
we make you a new one, each room

a different colour: a sea-green study
with its tiny computer glued to a paper shelf,

and the oriole-hued living room where
the black dog drowses on the couch,

and the rose kitchen trimmed with books
and stocked with whips of liquorice,

while through the swinging door
those you thought you'd lost

gather around the banquet table
circled by paper-thin walls which glow

like lanterns, walls about to ignite.
And of course, that's the point:

this house was made
for the next world. Still, we pause

here at the edge, willing the whole miracle
to stay a moment longer, this side of flame.

Irises

I'm awake in the night again,
asking which country, no, which
continent I'm in.

Floodlight like snow
blows against the barn door
and I'm travelling the land where

one brother brings warm water for hens
while the other pitches hay
to the heifer in her stall.

A fragment of dream
with morning on my baby son's skin
and irises blooming in snow

when the tingling begins,
then the letting-down
of blue streams, and once again

I'm as lonely
as long beds in winter gardens,
lonely as the hospital ward

where the city's crown
of blue jewelled lights
blinks like an apparition

wreathed by irises and prayers.
I drift, feeling that everyone is alone
but is going to be home

someday: the cow, the pony,
the Rhode Island Reds,
and even the poor souls

in the monastery gatehouse
– oh everything is full of yearning –
but at the centre of it,

a young mother drifts
and nurses her son among irises,
in the white falling world.